The outdoor Art Room

Summer

Rita Storey

W
FRANKLIN WATTS
LONDON SYDNEY

Franklin Watts
Published in Great Britain in paperback in 2018 by The Watts Publishing Group

Series editor: Sarah Peutrill
Art direction: Peter Scoulding
Series designed and created for Franklin Watts by Storeybooks
rita@storeybooks.co.uk
Designer: Rita Storey
Editor: Sarah Ridley
Photography: Tudor Photography, Banbury
Cover images: Tudor Photography, Banbury
Cover design: Cathryn Gilbert

ISBN 978 1 4451 4370 5

A CIP catalogue record for this book is available from the British Library.

Printed in China

MIX
Paper from responsible sources
FSC® C104740

Franklin Watts
An imprint of
Hachette Children's Group
Part of The Watts Publishing Group
Carmelite House
50 Victoria Embankment
London EC4Y 0DZ

An Hachette UK Company
www.hachette.co.uk

www.franklinwatts.co.uk

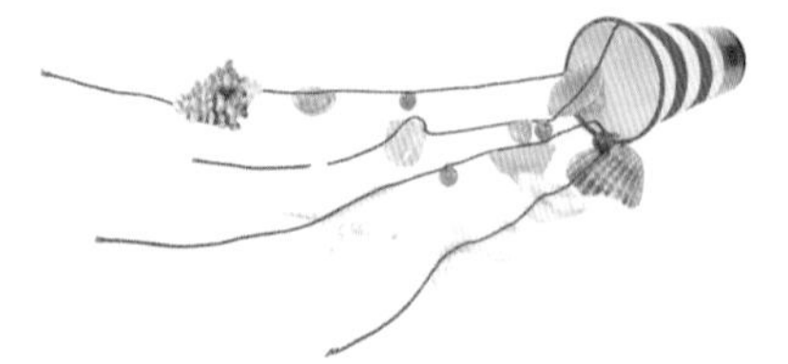

Before you start

Some of the projects in this book require scissors, strong glue, a kitchen knife and paints. When using these things we would recommend that children are supervised by a responsible adult.

Contents

All about summer

Summer is a wonderful time of the year to be in a garden, park or yard. This book is full of art projects and fun things to make and do outside. Have fun!

When is summer?

A year is the amount of time it takes for our planet Earth to go once around the sun. A year is divided into four seasons called spring, summer, autumn and winter. Summer occurs at different times of the year in different parts of the world. In the northern half of the world, summer lasts from June to August. In the southern half, it lasts from December to February. During the summer months, days are long and nights are short.

Summer is the hottest and sunniest season. We wear light clothing to keep cool. The rays from the sun can burn our skin. It is important to remember to wear sunscreen and a hat to avoid sunburn. In summer there is less rain. Sometimes it does not rain for weeks or even months, causing a drought. This can lead to water shortages and forest fires.

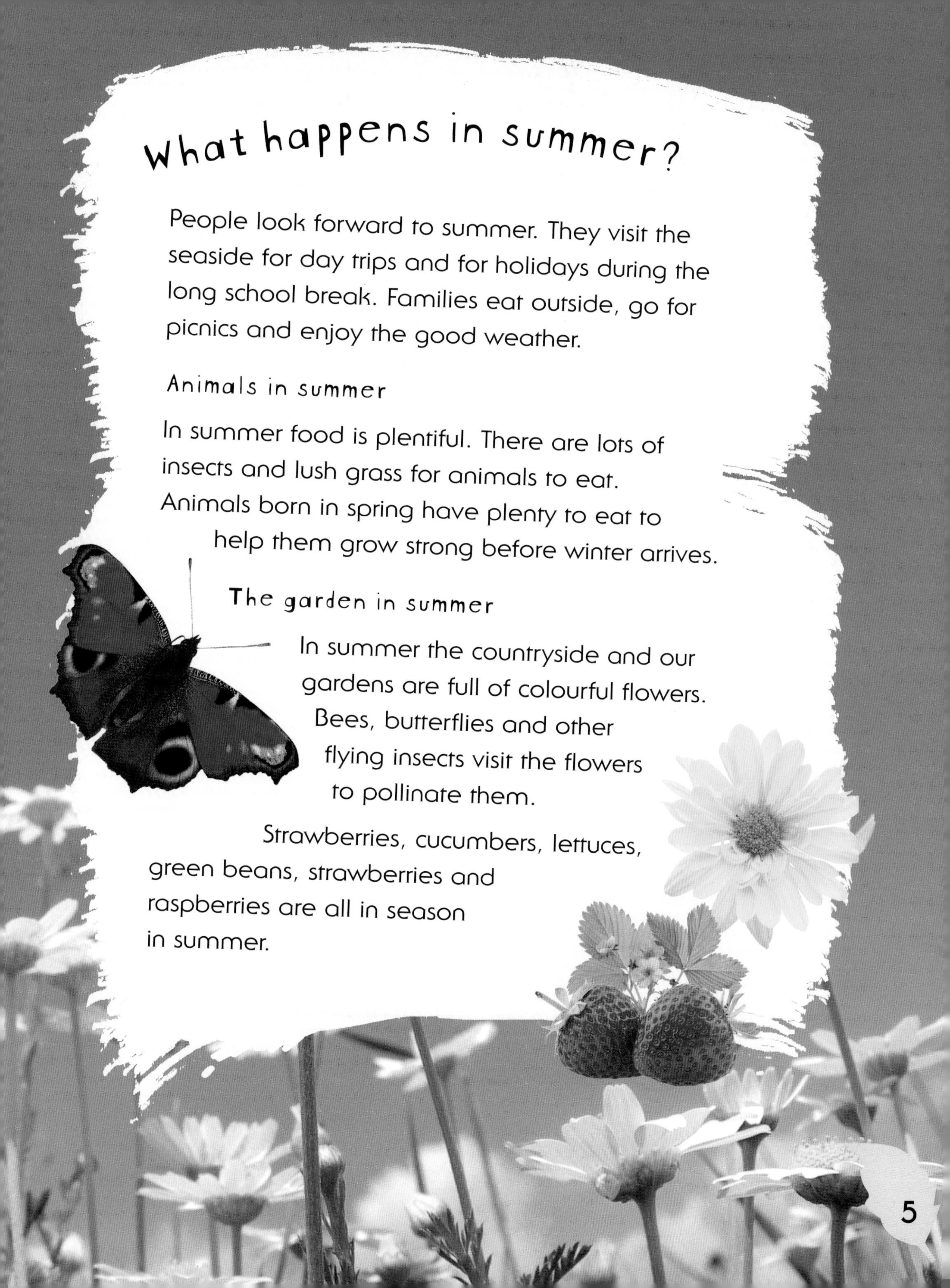

What happens in summer?

People look forward to summer. They visit the seaside for day trips and for holidays during the long school break. Families eat outside, go for picnics and enjoy the good weather.

Animals in summer

In summer food is plentiful. There are lots of insects and lush grass for animals to eat. Animals born in spring have plenty to eat to help them grow strong before winter arrives.

The garden in summer

In summer the countryside and our gardens are full of colourful flowers. Bees, butterflies and other flying insects visit the flowers to pollinate them.

Strawberries, cucumbers, lettuces, green beans, strawberries and raspberries are all in season in summer.

Shell mobile

On a trip to the seaside it is fun to collect shells. A great way to display them is to make them into a mobile. The shells on this mobile hang from a colourful homemade lighthouse.

1

Put a line of masking tape around the bottom, middle and top of the paper cup. Paint the cup red between the strips of tape and around the rim. Leave to dry.

You will need:

* white paper cup
* masking tape
* paintbrush and water container
* red paint
* scraps of black paper
* ruler
* scissors
* glue and spreader
* yellow pom-pom
* clear plastic cup (just the bottom 6cm)
* thick black felt-tip pen
* 1 piece of string, 20cm in length
* 4 pieces of string, 25cm in length
* seashells
* coloured beads
* strong glue

Peel off the strips of tape. Cut out two pieces of black paper 2cm x 3cm. Cut out one piece of black paper 4cm x 2.5cm. Glue them onto the cup as shown on the left.

Shell houses

Molluscs are a large group of animals with a soft body and no backbone. They include octopuses, slugs, snails, clams and limpets. Many types of mollusc have hard shells to protect them. Seashells that we find on the beach were once home to molluscs.

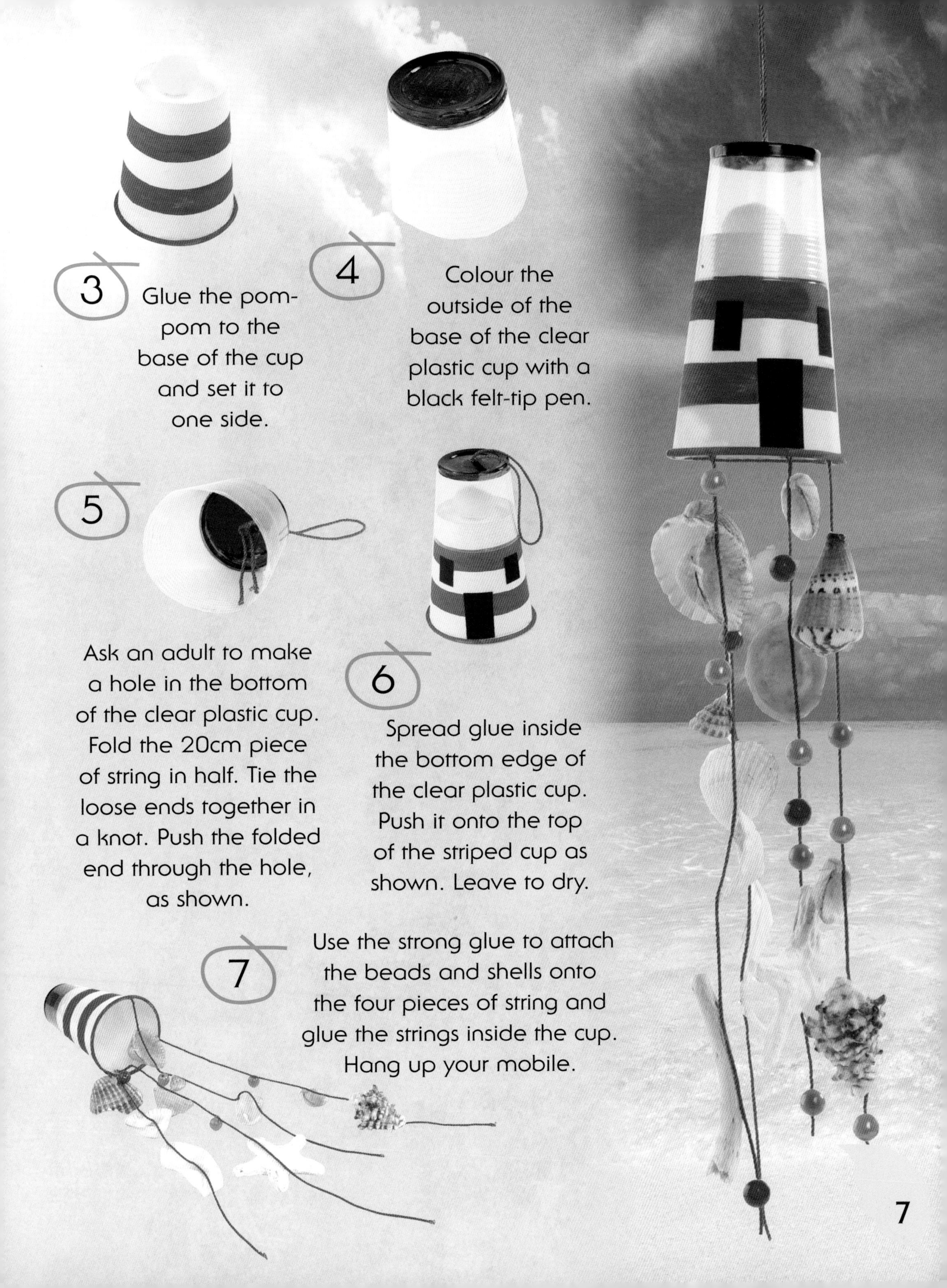

3 Glue the pom-pom to the base of the cup and set it to one side.

4 Colour the outside of the base of the clear plastic cup with a black felt-tip pen.

5 Ask an adult to make a hole in the bottom of the clear plastic cup. Fold the 20cm piece of string in half. Tie the loose ends together in a knot. Push the folded end through the hole, as shown.

6 Spread glue inside the bottom edge of the clear plastic cup. Push it onto the top of the striped cup as shown. Leave to dry.

7 Use the strong glue to attach the beads and shells onto the four pieces of string and glue the strings inside the cup. Hang up your mobile.

Flower bombs

On a hot day a water fight is a great way to cool down. These soft sponge flowers are great for drenching your friends.

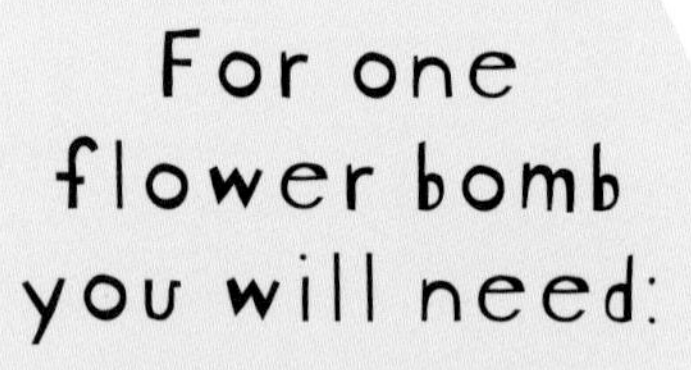

* 1cm-deep, blue sponge cloth
* 1cm-deep, pink sponge cloth
* 1cm-deep, yellow sponge cloth
* ruler
* scissors
* strong elastic band
* bowl
* water

1. Use scissors to cut three 1cm x 8cm strips from the blue sponge cloth. Repeat to cut strips from the pink and yellow sponges.

2. Lay strips of sponge cloth next to each other, as shown.

3. Put a layer of sponge strips on top, as shown.

4 Stack another layer of sponge strips on top, as shown.

5 Hold all the strips together and slip the elastic band over them.

6 Twist the elastic band until it is tight. Fluff out the ends. Make more flower bombs by repeating steps 1–6.

7 Dip the flower bombs into a bowl of water, divide them in half and find a friend who wants a water fight. Ready, steady, SPLASH!

Garden bunting

For an outdoor party, turn old comics, wrapping paper and garden string into colourful bunting to decorate your garden, playground or backyard.

You will need:

* pages from old comics and sheets of used wrapping paper
* scissors
* ruler
* pencil
* glue
* paintbrush or spreader
* ball of string

1. Cut the paper into strips that are 10cm wide x 30cm long.

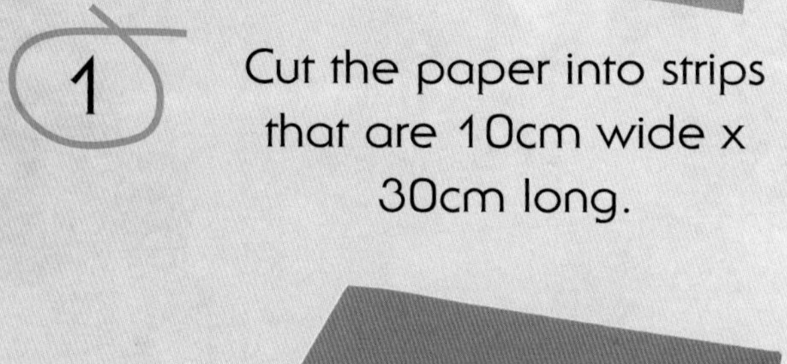

2. Fold each strip in half across its longest side. Make a mark with the pencil half way along the opposite edge to the fold.

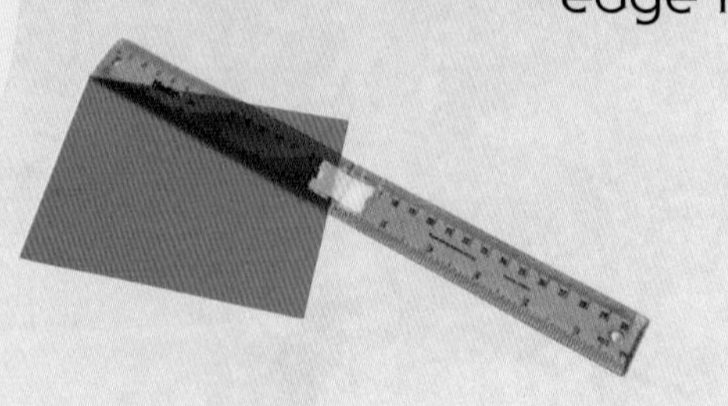

3. Draw a line from the pencil mark to the top left-hand corner of the folded edge.

4. Draw a line from the mark to the bottom left-hand corner of the folded edge.

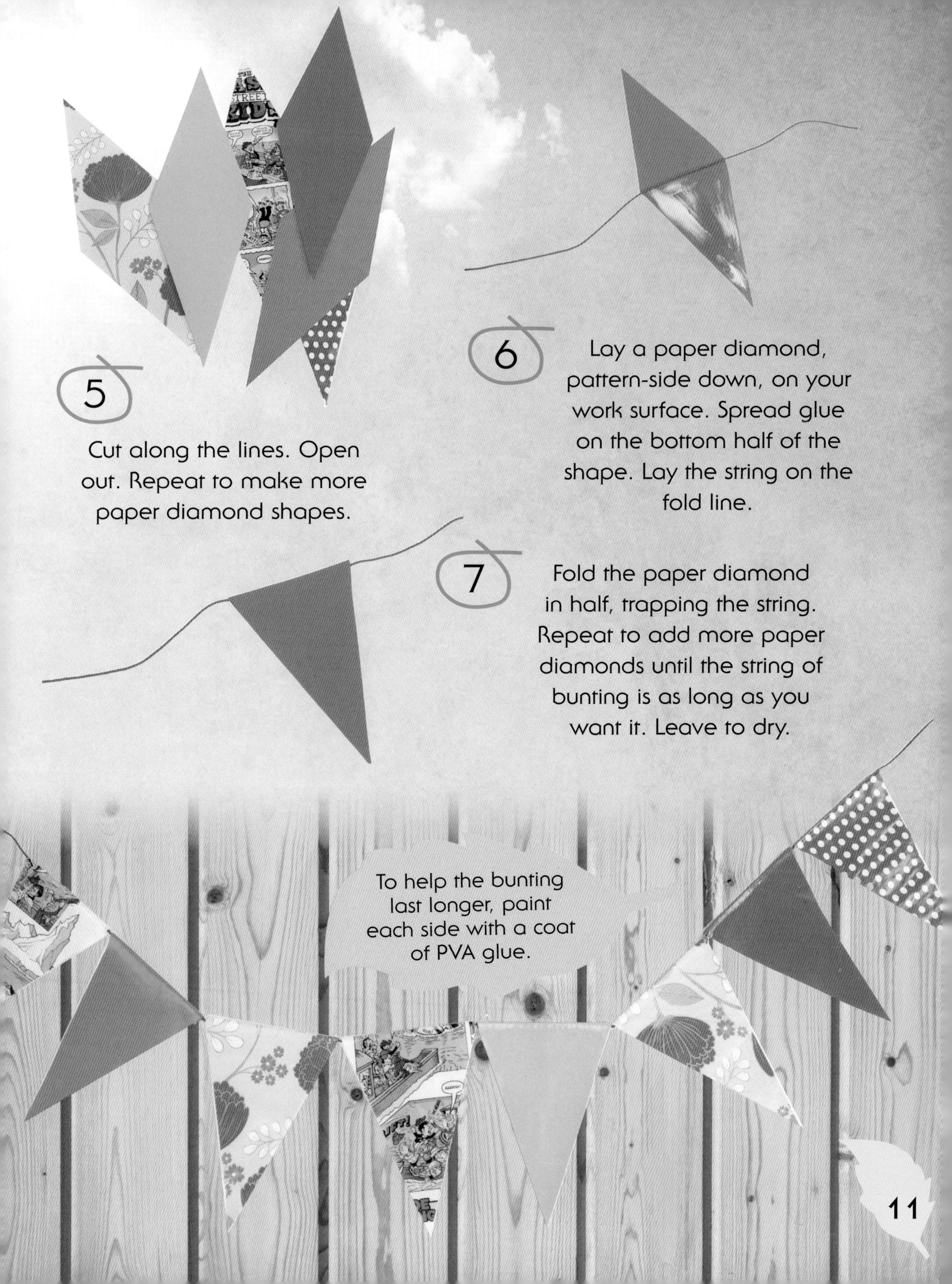

5

Cut along the lines. Open out. Repeat to make more paper diamond shapes.

6

Lay a paper diamond, pattern-side down, on your work surface. Spread glue on the bottom half of the shape. Lay the string on the fold line.

7

Fold the paper diamond in half, trapping the string. Repeat to add more paper diamonds until the string of bunting is as long as you want it. Leave to dry.

To help the bunting last longer, paint each side with a coat of PVA glue.

Water xylophone

Make this water xylophone and play it outside in the sunshine. Each bottle will make a slightly different sound when tapped with a spoon.

1. Use the pen and the ruler to mark a line 2cm from the base of a bottle. Place the funnel in the bottle and fill with water to the line.

You will need:

* 6 glass bottles or glasses the same size
* permanent marker pen
* ruler
* funnel
* jug of water
* food colouring (green, yellow, red, blue, purple and orange)
* metal spoon

2. 

Repeat to fill the other bottles with water after you have marked them as shown above.

3. Add a few drops of green food colouring to the bottle containing the most water.

Add different food colours to the rest of the bottles, as shown.

Write the numbers 1 to 6 on the bottles, starting with the bottle of green water. Make the numbers big.

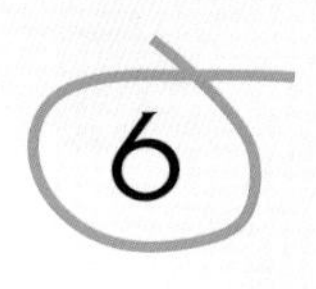

Gently tap the bottles with the spoon to play musical notes.

Play a tune by tapping the numbered bottles in different patterns, for instance: 1,2,3 – 2,3,1 – 1,2,3 – 2,3,1.

Sun print

Get outside on a sunny day and use the sunshine to make this stunning leaf print.

You will need:

* piece of white or cream cotton fabric, 80cm x 30cm
* plastic bowl with a small amount of water in it
* plastic bin liner
* acrylic paints mixed with the same amount of water
* paintbrush and water container
* a selection of leaves
* small stones

1 Make the fabric damp in the plastic bowl.

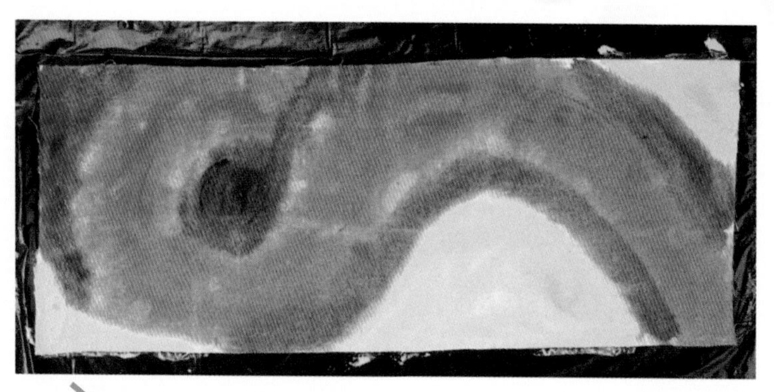

2 Lay the bin liner on the ground in full sunshine and spread out the wet fabric on top of it. Use the acrylic paints to create a swirling design.

3 Place the leaves on the painted fabric.

Sunlight

Light comes from the sun. Sunlight is a source of energy. It warms up the Earth and is used by plants to make food. During the summer the rays from the sun are at their strongest.

4. Stop the leaves from moving by placing some small stones on top of them. Leave everything in the sunshine for a few hours until the fabric is completely dry.

The fabric under the objects will dry more slowly than the fabric exposed to the sunlight. The areas that dry more quickly pull the paint from under the objects, leaving paler shapes.

5. Peel off the leaves to reveal their shapes.

Very flat leaves work best. Or you could try some other flat objects such as garden tools or stones.

Fairy ring

Many children's books show pictures of fairies dancing inside a ring of colourful toadstools on a summer evening. Make a ring of toadstools for your garden and imagine fairies dancing inside it.

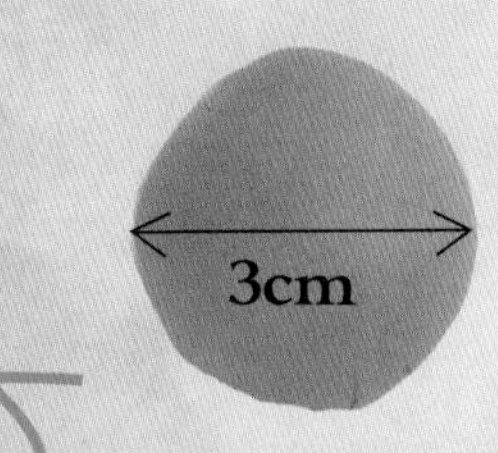

1. Roll the clay into six balls, measuring about 3cm across the widest part.

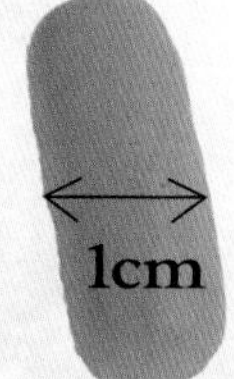

2. Roll out a long sausage of clay 1cm across. Using the kitchen knife, cut six pieces from the clay sausage, each about 2.5cm long.

3. Press your fingers into the balls of clay to make dish shapes like the one in the picture.

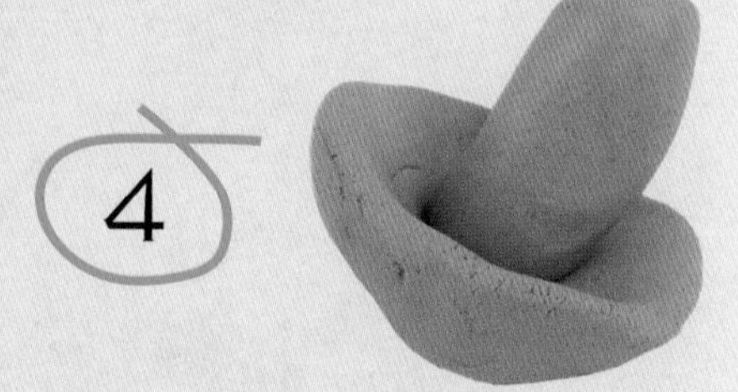

4. Paint some water onto one end of each piece. Press the wet end into the centre of each clay dish to make a toadstool shape.

You will need:

* 500gm air-dry clay
* ruler
* kitchen knife
* paintbrush and water container
* white, red, yellow and blue acrylic craft paint

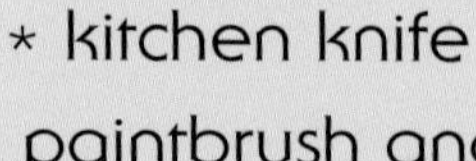

5. Paint the clay toadstools white. Leave them to dry.

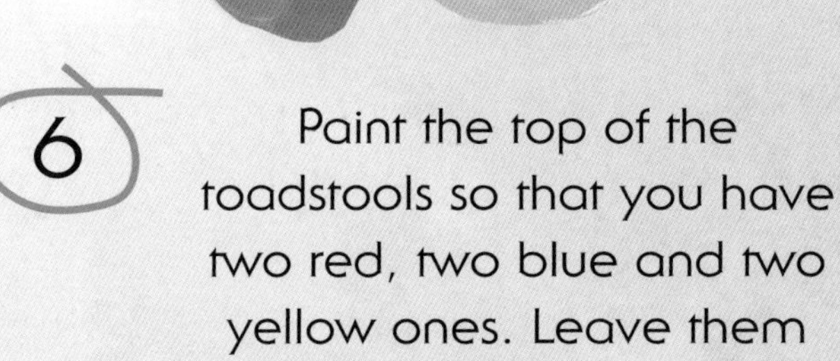

6. Paint the top of the toadstools so that you have two red, two blue and two yellow ones. Leave them to dry.

7. Paint on white spots and leave them to dry.

To keep the toadstools looking bright, take them inside if it looks like rain.

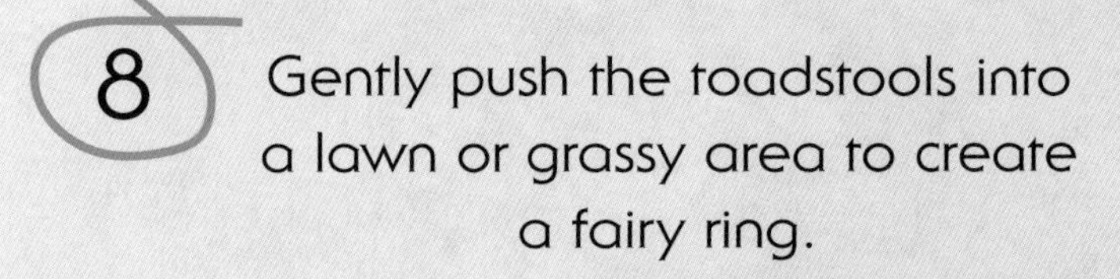

8. Gently push the toadstools into a lawn or grassy area to create a fairy ring.

Sunflower race

Sunflowers are a wonderful sight in late summer. They can grow very tall. Work out which is the tallest sunflower using this colourful ladybird measuring stick.

You will need:

* packet of sunflower seeds (and flowerpots if you need them)
* pencil and thin white paper (for tracing the templates)
* scissors
* A4 sheet of orange craft foam
* sewing pin
* A4 sheet of black craft foam
* latex glue and spreader
* 7cm piece of black pipe cleaner
* 2 googly eyes
* scraps of blue, yellow, green and black craft foam
* measuring tape
* long garden cane
* paintbrush and coloured paints
* black felt-tip pen

Sow the sunflower seeds in your garden or in large flowerpots, following the instructions on the seed packet. Remember to water your sunflowers as they grow.

2

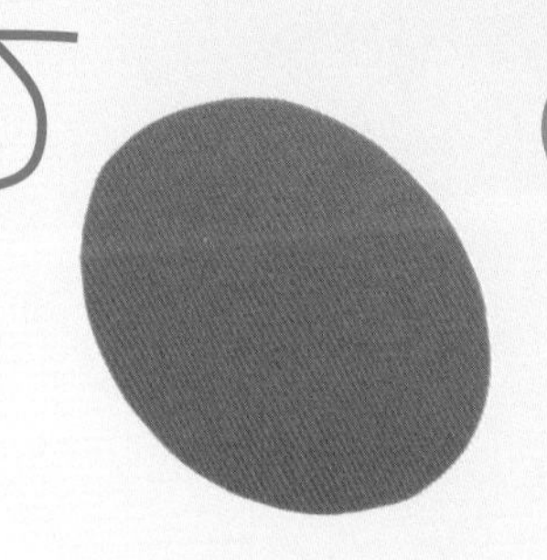

Use the white paper to trace and cut out the oval template on page 31. Pin it to the orange craft foam and cut out the ladybird body.

3

Trace and cut out the semicircle template on page 31. Pin it to the black craft foam and cut around it. Glue the black foam to the orange ladybird body, as shown.

Fold the piece of black pipe cleaner in half. Curl the ends round as shown in the picture below. Glue it to the back of the ladybird body.

5

Ask an adult to cut two slits in the ladybird body as shown here. Glue on two googly eyes. Use the templates on page 31 to cut out spots from the craft foam scraps and glue them on. Leave to dry.

6

Use the measuring tape and pen to make marks every 10cm along the garden cane. Paint each 10cm section a different colour. When the paint has dried, use the pen to write all the numbers to create a measuring stick.

Slide the foam ladybird onto the garden cane.

Slide the ladybird up the stick as the sunflowers grow. Which sunflower will win?

In dry weather, water the sunflowers every day.

Minibeast detective

In summer, minibeasts like a cool, dark place to hide from the sun. Attract some of them to your minibeast hotel.

You will need:

* flowerpot
* a small stone
* leaves * sticks
* a flat stone
* half an orange
* teaspoon
* paintbrush
* paper cups
* pen
* notebook
* magnifying glass

Choose a sheltered spot in semi-shade. Place the flowerpot upside down, using a small stone to lift up one edge so that minibeasts can crawl inside.

2

Pile up some leaves and sticks next to the flowerpot.

3

Scoop the middle out of half an orange with a teaspoon. Place it next to the flowerpot with its cut side down. Make sure minibeasts can crawl inside it.

Put a flat stone next to the flowerpot, leaves and orange.
Leave your new minibeast hotel for a few days.

Minibeasts

Minibeasts are small animals that don't have backbones. They include spiders, slugs, worms, beetles, centipedes, snails, earwigs, woodlice and caterpillars.

5 Draw a grid like this one in your notebook.

Take the minibeast hotel apart. Use the paintbrush to brush the minibeasts into paper cups. Look very carefully at what you have collected. Count how many of each minibeast there are. Fill in the grid.

When you have counted the minibeasts, gently release them back into the wild close to where you had your minibeast hotel.

It is best to keep different types of minibeast apart so that they do not attack each other.

Bees and daisies game

This outdoor game for two players follows the same rules as noughts and crosses. Use the bees instead of noughts and the flowers instead of crosses.

You will need:

* 5 oval stones
* yellow, black and white acrylic craft paint
* paintbrush
* jam jar of water (to wash your paintbrush clean)
* 5 round stones
* piece of chalk

1 Paint three yellow stripes on an oval stone. Leave to dry.

2 Paint three black stripes between the yellow stripes. Leave to dry.

3 Use white paint to paint two eyes and a pair of wings.

Bees

In summer bees collect nectar from flowers. They take the nectar back to their hive or nest. The nectar collected by all the bees is turned into honey.

4 Paint a yellow spot in the centre of a round stone.

5 Paint white petals around the yellow circle, as shown. Leave to dry.

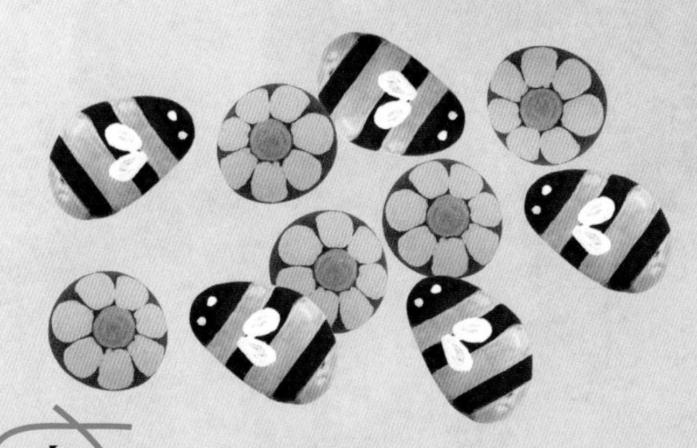

6 Repeat steps 1–5 to make five bee stones and five daisy stones.

7 Draw chalk lines on a paving stone, concrete or tarmac area, copying this pattern.

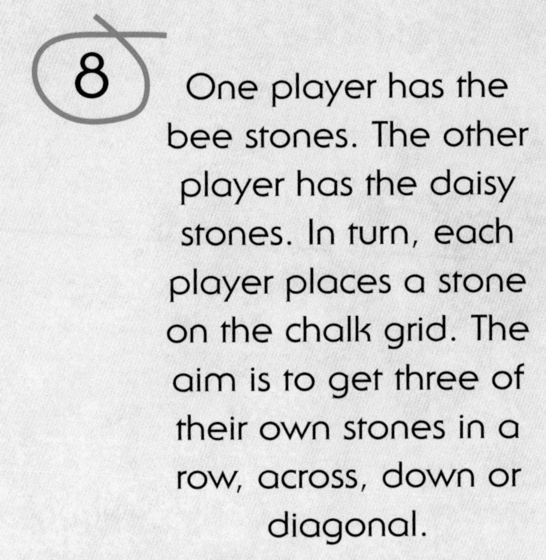

8 One player has the bee stones. The other player has the daisy stones. In turn, each player places a stone on the chalk grid. The aim is to get three of their own stones in a row, across, down or diagonal.

Rose perfume

Many roses smell beautiful. This rose-scented perfume is the smell of summer for many people!

You will need:

* scented rose
* small jar
* water
* sieve and bowl
* funnel
* small bottle with lid
* sticky label, coloured felt-tip pens and ribbon to decorate

1. Ask an adult's permission to cut a rose from their garden. Choose a rose with a strong scent.

2. Gently pull the petals off the rose.

3. Put the petals into the jar and fill the jar with water.

Flowers

Some flowers use scent to attract butterflies, bees and other flying insects. The insects help to pollinate the flowers by carrying pollen from flower to flower.

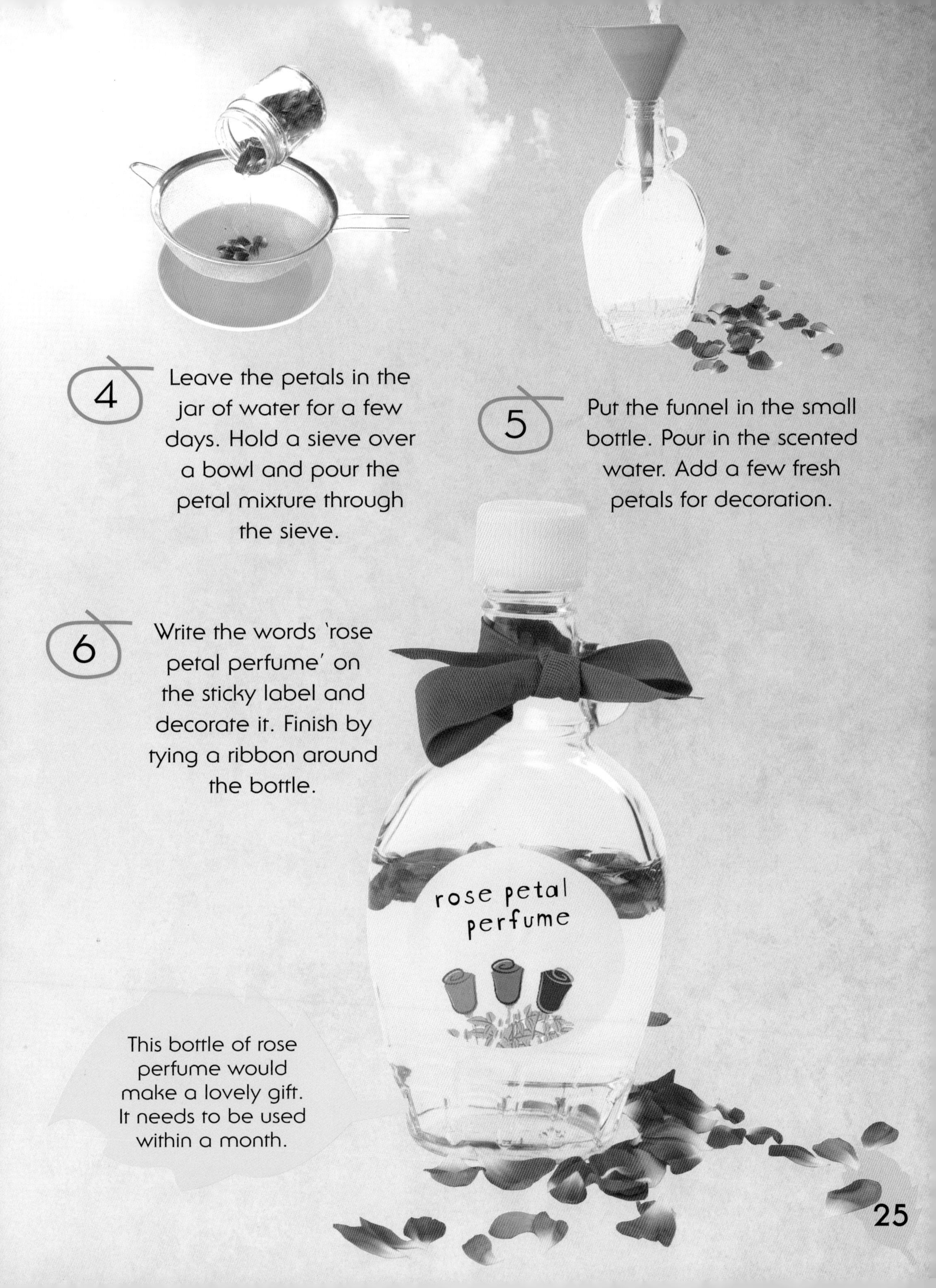

4 Leave the petals in the jar of water for a few days. Hold a sieve over a bowl and pour the petal mixture through the sieve.

5 Put the funnel in the small bottle. Pour in the scented water. Add a few fresh petals for decoration.

6 Write the words 'rose petal perfume' on the sticky label and decorate it. Finish by tying a ribbon around the bottle.

This bottle of rose perfume would make a lovely gift. It needs to be used within a month.

Flower print picture

Making a colourful flower print picture using real flowers is very easy. The printed paper makes great wrapping paper too.

Take the largest flower. Dip the brush into the pink paint. Brush the flower petals with paint.

You will need:

* flowers with a flat flower head (1 large, 2 medium and 1 small). Ask permission before cutting flowers.
* paintbrush and water container for cleaning
* pink, yellow, purple and blue paint
* sheet of A3 white paper

Press the flower head onto the paper to make a print. Carefully lift the flower head and use it to make more prints on different parts of the paper. Leave to dry.

Select one of the medium-sized flowers and brush its petals with yellow paint.

Colourful flowers

Flower petals are brightly coloured so that they attract butterflies, bees and other insects flying above them.

4 Print the flower onto the white paper several times. Leave to dry.

5 Repeat steps 1–4 with the small flower head and purple paint. Leave to dry. Repeat steps 1–4 with the other medium-sized flower head and the blue paint.

Instead of printing the flower heads all over the paper, try making a pattern with them.

Butterfly feeder

Butterflies feed on the nectar from flowers. You can attract butterflies into your garden by feeding them homemade nectar.

You will need:

* pencil and thin white paper (for tracing the template)
* scissors
* sewing pin
* A4 sheets of yellow, purple and orange craft foam
* 3 pipe cleaners (green, purple and orange)
* latex glue and spreader
* plastic bottle cap
* 1 tbsp sugar dissolved in 142ml/5floz water
* cotton wool balls
* plastic garden stick

Use the pencil and paper to trace the template on page 31 and cut it out. Lay it on the yellow foam, pin in place and trace around it using a pencil.

Cut out the foam flower shape.

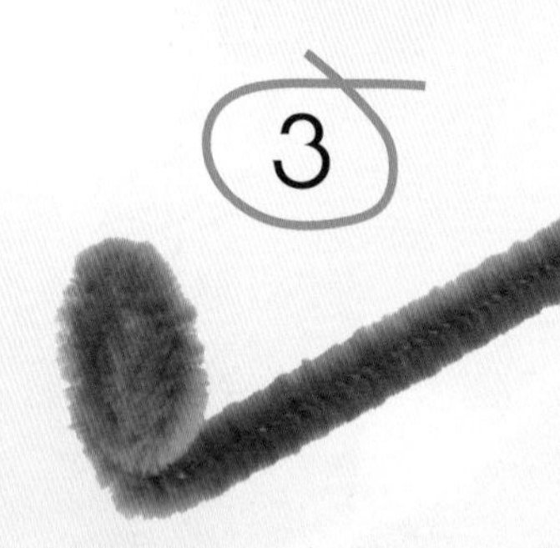

3. Twist the end of the green pipe cleaner into a spiral as shown.

Spread glue onto the end of the pipe cleaner. Press it onto the foam flower. Leave to dry.

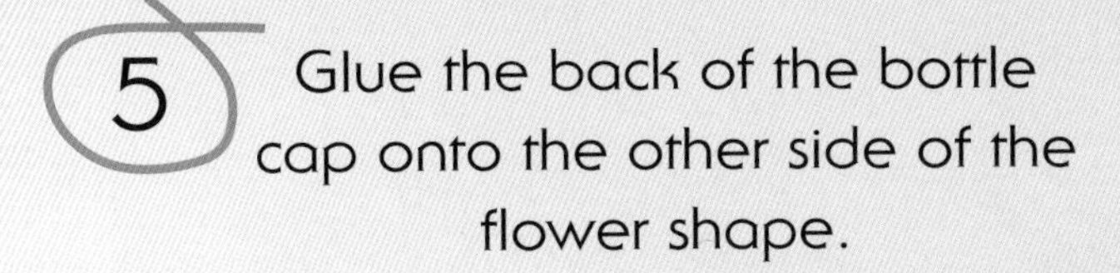

5 Glue the back of the bottle cap onto the other side of the flower shape.

6 Soak a cotton wool ball in the sugar and water syrup. Push the soaked cotton wool ball into the bottle cap.

7 Repeat steps 1–6 to make two more flowers using the orange and then the purple craft foam. Twist the pipe cleaner stems around the garden stick.

8 Choose a sunny spot and push the stick into the ground in your garden or in a plant container. Return to the feeder every hour or so to see if butterflies have discovered your feeder.

Butterflies

A butterfly has four different stages to its lifecycle: egg, caterpillar, pupa and butterfly.

Peacock butterflies lay their eggs on nettles in spring. These hatch into caterpillars 10 days later. The caterpillars feed on the nettles and then change into pupa, emerging as butterflies in summer.

Keep the rest of the sugar syrup in a bottle to top up the feeder.

Summer words

caterpillar the young of a butterfly or moth

drought a long period of time without rainfall

fertilise in plants, when the male and female part of a plant join together to make seeds

hive a shelter for a colony of bees

in season the time of year when a fruit or vegetable is ripe and plentiful

insect a small animal that has three parts to its body, six legs and often has two pairs of wings

lifecycle the series of changes in the life of an animal or plant

nectar a sweet liquid produced in a flower

petal the colourful part of a flower

pollen a fine powder found on flowers

pollinate the way pollen is moved from one plant to another to fertilise it so that it can make seeds

pupa the stage of an insect's lifecycle between the young and the adult

scent a strong smell

seed the part of a plant that grows into a new plant

sunlight light from the sun, which travels in straight lines, also called rays

sunscreen a cream or liquid that protects the skin from invisible, harmful sun rays

toadstool the fruit of a fungus, also called a mushroom

Templates

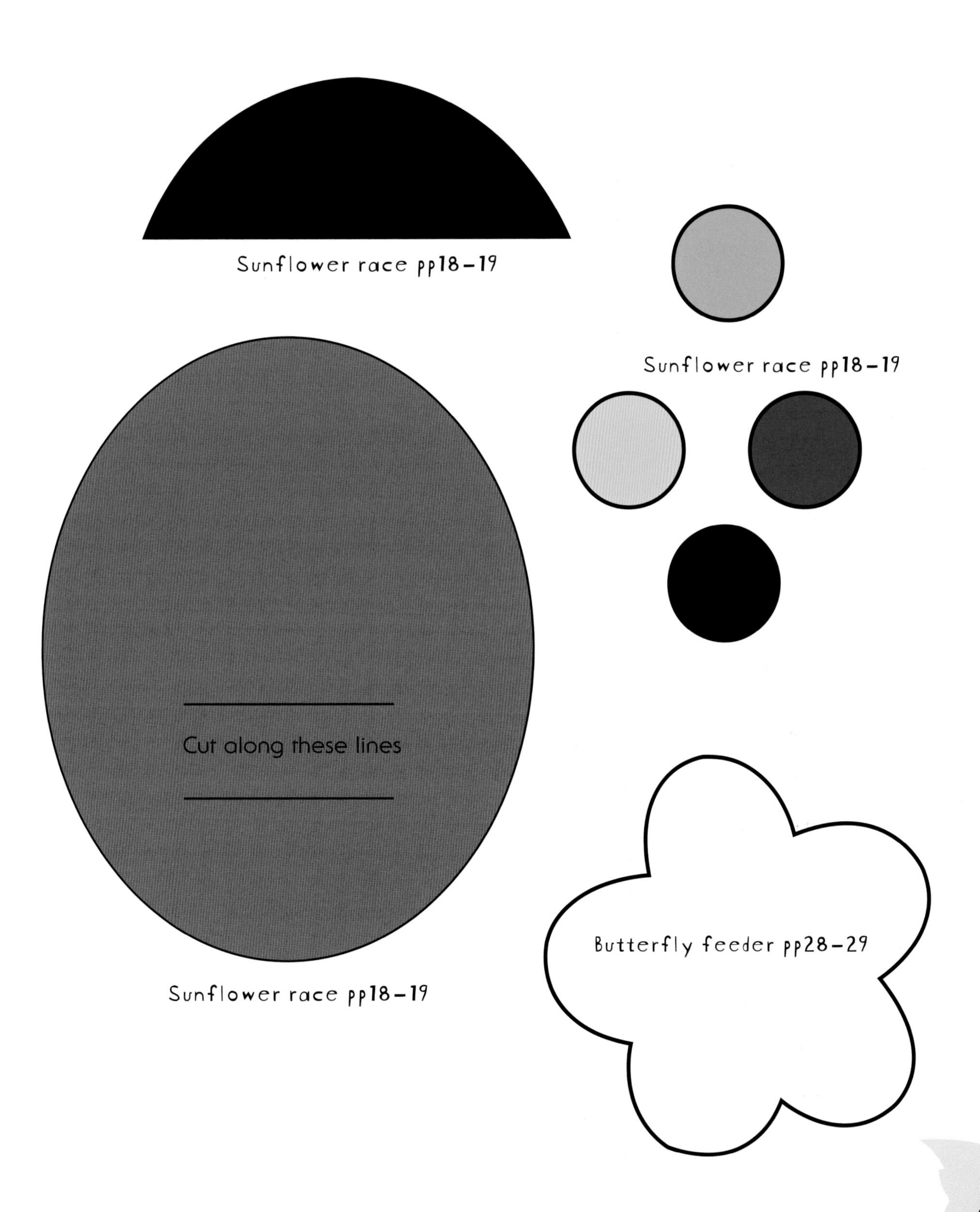
Sunflower race pp18–19
Sunflower race pp18–19
Cut along these lines
Sunflower race pp18–19
Butterfly feeder pp28–29

Index

Find out more

www.dltk-holidays.com/summer/index.html
Lots of great summer themed crafts and activities.

www.woodlandtrust.org.uk/naturedetectives/
Activities from the Woodland Trust.

www.bbc.co.uk/guides/zcx3gk7
BBC guide to the seasons.

www.education.com/slideshow/summer-science-activities/
Great science projects for summer days.